Copyright © 2021 by Zeinab Shalaby.

All Rights Reserved. No part of this book may be reproduced, transmitted, or stored in an information retrieval system in any form or by any means, graphic, electronic, or mechanical, including photocopying, taping, and recording, without prior written permission from the publisher.

First edition 2021
ISBN 978-1-7357701-3-0
Edited by Noha Elmouelhi

Published by Honey Elm Books LLC
www.HoneyElmBooks.com

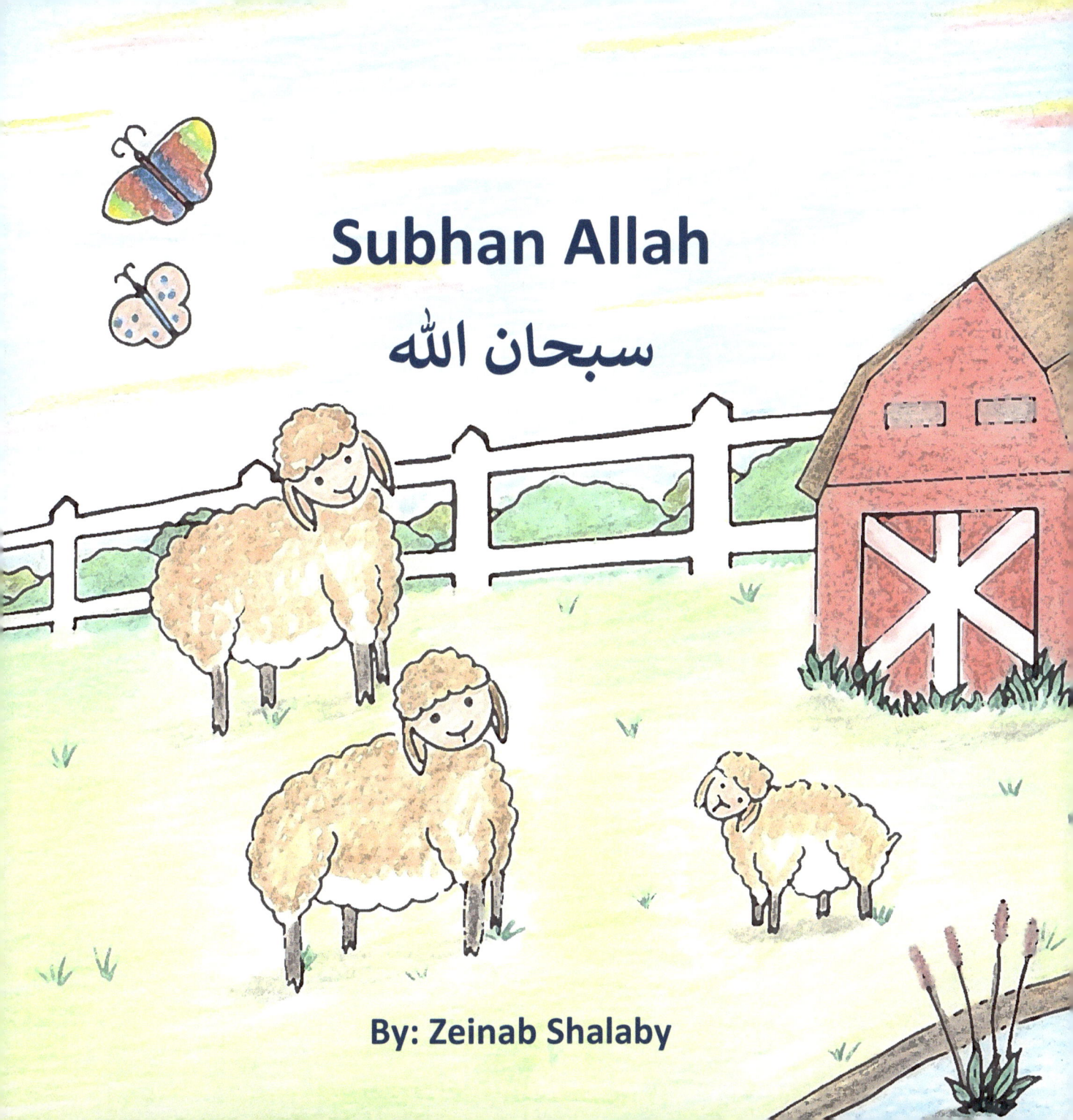

**Look at the turtle
   with its big, hard shell...**

Look at all the fish...

Look at the sun

shining so bright...

www.ingramcontent.com/pod-product-compliance
Lightning Source LLC
Chambersburg PA
CBHW042256100526
44589CB00002B/48